NATIONAL LAMPOON

★ ★ ★ ★ ★ ★

How
Dumb
Are
You ?

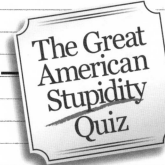

The Great
American
Stupidity
Quiz

By Adam Winer

Design by TK Creative
Research assistance by Kate Miltner
Special thanks to the vigorously awesome readers of BWE.tv

Published by National Lampoon Press

National Lampoon, Inc. • 8228 Sunset Boulevard • Los Angeles • CA 90046 • USA

AMEX:NLN

NATIONAL LAMPOON, NATIONAL LAMPOON PRESS and colophon are trademarks of National Lampoon

National lampoon, How dumb are you? The great american stupidity quiz
/ by Adam Winer -- 1st ed.

p. cm.

ISBN-10: 0980059208
ISBN-13: 978-0980059205 - $9.99

Book Design by
TK Creative

1   3   5   7   9   10   8   6   4   2

MAY 2008

WWW.NATIONALLAMPOON.COM

To mom and dad,
the two most undumbest people I know.

From the Noted Author

Dear People Who Think They're Smart,

Your self-esteem is adorable. Unfortunately, this book was created to crush it.

Let's be clear, I'm not here to say you're dumb. I'm just here to say you're *probably* dumb. Certainly dumber than you give yourself credit for. To achieve a better understanding of your overall mental failings and actually measure the exact level of your stupidity, take the quiz in this book. It's made of questions that you *should* know the answers to—but often don't.

The setup of the book is so simple even you'll understand it. On the right-hand pages, you'll find the questions. Attempt to wrap your mind around each one, then flip the page to find the answer. On the answer pages, you'll also find a related Fun Fact. Memorize these Fun Facts, then later throw them out in casual conversation. They'll help you trick people into thinking you're actually smart!

Now onto a word about scoring: This quiz has already been inflicted upon a test audience. A box on each answer page reveals what percentage of these average citizens got the question correct. By consulting these stats, you'll be able to see, on a question-by-question basis, exactly how poorly you stack up against your fellow Americans.

Once you've completed the entire quiz, count how many questions you answered incorrectly. Then consult the scoring section at book's end for an overarching assessment of your state of ignorance. Hint: If, at any point, your lips were moving as you read this page to yourself, you're already in trouble.

Still with me? Good job. Now let's get stupid.

Adam Winer

Question 1

Here's a map of the U.S. ★★★

★★★

Which state is Nebraska?

>Nebraska

★ ★ ★

If you got this wrong, you are dumber than

73%

of America!

FUN FACTS

None of the members of Nebraska's state Legislature are Republicans or Democrats because the state constitution bans all political affiliations in that local body. That makes the Cornhuskers the only folks in the country to have actually made partisanship illegal.

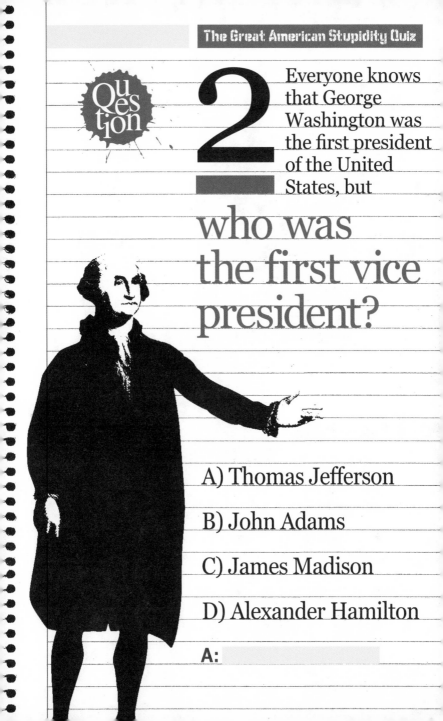

Question

2

Everyone knows that George Washington was the first president of the United States, but

who was the first vice president?

A) Thomas Jefferson

B) John Adams

C) James Madison

D) Alexander Hamilton

A:

John Adams

If you got this wrong, you are dumber than

 **%**

of America!

FUN FACTS

Until 1804, the vice presidency went to the presidential candidate who came in second in the electoral-college voting, kind of like the country's biggest consolation prize. That meant sometimes the P and VP were rivals. John Adams, for example, often called George Washington "Old Muttonhead." It was said affectionately, no doubt.

Question

3

Longitude & latitude:

Which one runs up & down?

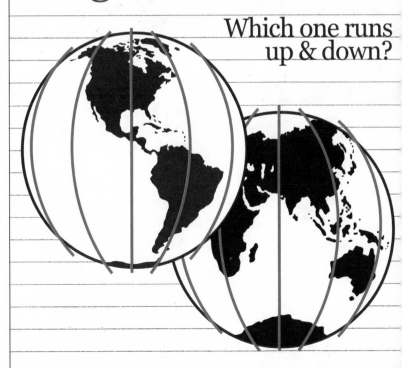

Longitude

★ ★ ★

D

If you got this wrong, you are dumber than

72%

of America!

FUN FACTS

Each degree of latitude is 69 miles apart. Similarly, at the equator, each degree of longitude is 69 miles apart. That's right, both are 69. Whoever created that system was totally kinky. We're looking at you, Britain.

Question

4

Mozart

is one of the most famous composers in history. Can you remember his full name?

A:

Wolfgang Amadeus Mozart

If you got this wrong, you are dumber than 67% of America!

FUN FACTS

In addition to his lofty symphonies and operas, Mozart also enjoyed making cruder compositions. For example, he once wrote rounds (a.k.a. musical setups like "Row, Row, Row Your Boat") for the words "Leck mich im arsch"—which roughly translates to "Lick me in the ass"—and "Leck mir den arsch fein recht schon sauber." That would be, "Lick me in the ass nice and clean."

This is a dime.

5

Who is the dude on it?

A:

★ ★ ★ **Answer** ★ ★ ★

Franklin D. Rsevelt

>

D ★

If you got this
wrong, you are
dumber than

%

of America!

FUN FACTS

Franklin D. Roosevelt's fifth cousin
was President Theodore Roosevelt.
And Teddy's niece was Eleanor
Roosevelt. That means—yup—FDR
ended up marrying a distant
cousin. A little creepy, sure, but
on the bright side, Eleanor never
had to go through the headache of
changing her last name.

Question **6**

★ ★ ★

What is the capital of Canada?

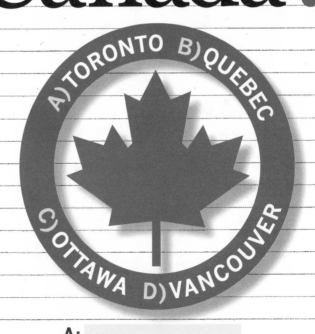

A)TORONTO B)QUEBEC C)OTTAWA D)VANCOUVER

A:

>

Toronto

Quebec

Ottawa ✓

Vancouver

★ ★ ★

If you got this wrong, you are dumber than

57%

of America!

FUN FACTS

Although Canada is the second largest country in the world in area (behind Russia), it's peppered with only 32 million residents. So on the inevitable day when it finally just gives up being its own country and becomes one of our states, it will still have fewer people than California.

Question

7

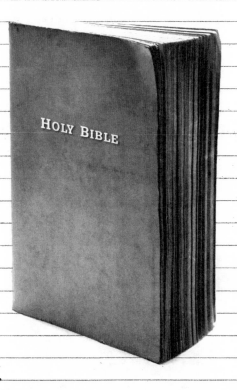

HOLY BIBLE

Thousands of years ago, God gave Charlton Heston 10 commandments.

Can you name even half of The Bible's Ten Commandments?

> 1. I am the Lord your God, thou shall have no other gods before me. Plus, lay off those false idols.*

Ans wer

> 2. Thou shall not take the name of the Lord in vain.

> 3. Remember the Sabbath and keep it holy.

> 4. Honour thy father and mother.

> 5. Thou shall not kill.

> 6. Thou shall not commit adultery.

> 7. Thou shall not steal.

> 8. Thou shall not bear false witness against thy neighbor.

> 9. Thou shall not covet thy neighbor's wife.

> 10. Thou shall not covet thy neighbor's ox or ass (or any of his other stuff).

*Depending on your religion, this may have been considered two separate commandments. (And 9 and 10 were lumped together as one.) Feel free to score thyself appropriately.

D

If you got this wrong, you are dumber than

%

of America!

FUN FACTS

Remember that famous scene in *The Ten Commandments* when Charlton Heston parts the Red Sea? To create it, director Cecil B. DeMille filmed water flooding *into* a dry riverbed. He then ran that footage in reverse.

Question 8

Please define:

What is a prime number?

A:

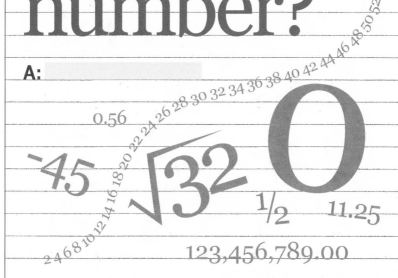

A number that's only divisible by 1 & itself.

Answer

★ ★ ★

2 3 5 7 11 13 17 19 . . .

If you got this wrong, you are dumber than

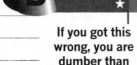

71%

of America!

FUN FACTS

Mathematicians nerd out on finding ridiculously huge prime numbers. The largest prime number currently known to exist measures 9.8 million digits long and was discovered by a group of networked computers. We would write the number here, except it would take up all the space in this book—along with all the space in all the other books on the shelf.

9

Forget trying to remember
which four presidents
are on Mt. Rushmore.

Do you even know
what state the
monument is in?

A:

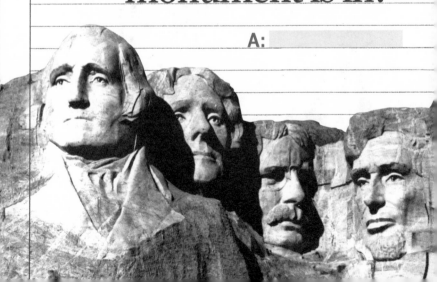

South Dakota

Answer

If you got this wrong, you are dumber than

61%

of America!

FUN FACTS

Thomas Jefferson's head was first sculpted to the left of George Washington, but chief chiseler Gutzon Borglum didn't think the face looked enough like Jefferson—so he blew it away with dynamite. Borglum then resculpted TJ to the right of Washington, but even then some early tourists mistook Jefferson for Martha Washington.

Question

10

Why should you know who this guy is?

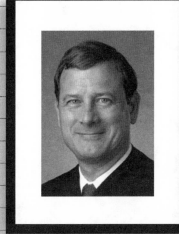

A:

That is

John Roberts

Chief Justice of the Supreme Court.

That makes him, like, the president of judges.

Kinda.

★ ★ ★

If you got this wrong, you are dumber than

%

of America!

FUN FACTS

The Constitution doesn't dictate how many justices should be on the Supreme Court. In fact, the original court had only six judges. Over the Supreme's first hundred years, Congress jimmied with its size seven times, until finally deciding they liked the group picture best when it was made up of nine old white guys in black robes.

Remember how you learned what an adverb was in, like, second grade?

Which of these words is an adverb?

A) Ignorant

B) Stammering

C) Stupidly

D) Nincompoop

A:

Ignorant

Stammering

Stupidly ✔

Nincompoop

An adverb is a word that modifies a verb, adjective, clause or other adverb. When you were 8, they taught you that usually meant the word ended in -ly.

★ ★ ★

If you got this wrong, you are dumber than

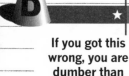

81%

of America!

FUN FACTS

Good writers tend to loathe adverbs. Nobel Prize winner Gabriel García Márquez declared that his 1983 novel *Chronicle of a Death Foretold* contained only one adverb, and then swore he'd never use another one again. Feel free to go through his later works and double-check—if you have way too much time on your hands.

12

Question

There are Seven Wonders of the Ancient World. Name Two.

A:

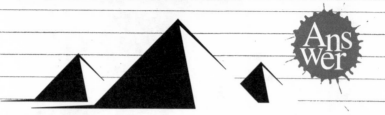

Answer

> Pyramids of Giza
> Temple of Artemis at Ephesus
> Hanging Gardens of Babylon
> Statue of Zeus at Olympia
> Mausoleum at Halicarnassus
> Colossus of Rhodes
> Pharos (Lighthouse) at Alexandria

★ ★ ★

If you got this wrong, you are dumber than

30%

of America!

FUN FACTS

The walls of Babylon and the palace of King Cyrus of Persia were included on some early Lists-O-Wonders, but eventually fell off. All the record keeping was done by the Greeks. This explains why a list that is billed as the Seven Wonders of the *World* contains only monuments within a convenient chariot hop from Greece.

Question

13

Since 9/11, the U.S. has launched major military actions in both Iraq & Afghanistan.

Can you find either one of those countries on this map?

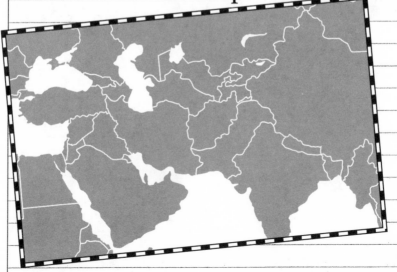

Iraq
Afghanistan

★ ★ ★

If you got this wrong, you are dumber than

61 %

of America!

FUN FACTS

During their stint ruling Afghanistan, the Taliban outlawed kite flying, playing the drums, dancing at weddings and clapping during sporting events. Oh, and sorcery. They also outlawed sorcery. Good thing they didn't forget that one.

Qu es tion

Without touching your chest:

What side of your body is your heart on?

14

A:

It's centered but off a little to your left.

★ ★ ★

Ans wer

If you got this wrong, you are **dumber than** **84**% **of America!**

FUN FACTS

An adult heart beats about 75 times per minute, and squirts roughly 2.5 ounces of blood every beat. Add up all that pumping, and you find that, in a single day, the heart processes 2,500 gallons of blood, with a total weight of roughly 20 tons.

15

How many Quarts are in a Gallon?

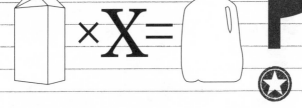

A:

Four

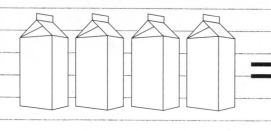

★ ★ ★

If you got this wrong, you are dumber than

60%

of America!

FUN FACTS

There are two pints in a quart. And how much does a pint of water weigh? Well, they say, "A pint is a pound the world around." But that saying's wrong. In the U.S., a pint is 16 fl. oz, but it's 20 fl. oz in the rest of the world. Hence the new saying: "A pint of water weighs a pound and a quarter." It's less catchy, but more accurate.

Qestion

16

Which historic
U.S. document
begins,

"We the People
of the
United States..."

A) The Declaration of Independence   B) The Constitution

★ ★ ★

B)

The Constitution

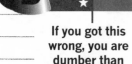

We the People *of the United*

insure domestic Tranquility, provide for the common defence, promote the
and our Posterity, do ordain and establish this Constitution for the United S

Article. I.

All legislative Powers herein granted, shall be vested in a Con
ri slives.

1. The House of Representatives shall be composed of Members ch
shall have Qualifications requisite for Electors of the most numerous B

If you got this wrong, you are dumber than

40%

of America!

FUN FACTS

Those famous words were actually a rewrite. Initially, the wording was: "We the people of the states of New Hampshire, Massachusetts..." It was changed because no one knew if every state would actually ratify the new Constitution. Rhode Island, for example, even refused to send delegates to the convention that wrote it.

Question 17

Who wrote the book
War and
Peace?

A:

Ans wer

Leo
> Tolstoy

★ ★ ★

If you got this wrong, you are dumber than

50%

of America!

FUN FACTS

Tolstoy gets all the credit for writing *War and Peace*, but his put-upon wife, Sofya, deserves a shout-out as well. It was Sofya's job to take Leo's nearly illegible manuscript for the 1,400-page book and neatly recopy it... seven times.

There was a time not too long ago when the USSR was our enemy.

Any idea what the letters USSR stood for?

A:

Union of Soviet Socialist Republics

★ ★ ★

If you got this wrong, you are dumber than

29%

of America!

FUN FACTS

Vladimir Lenin was the first leader of the Soviet Union, with Leon Trotsky as his number two. After Lenin died, Big Joe Stalin pushed his way into power and banished Trotsky from the country. Later, Stalin decided banishment wasn't enough, so a Russian agent tracked Trotsky to his new home in Mexico. And drove an ice ax into his skull.

Question

19

What were the names of **Christopher Columbus's ships?**

A:

🚢 The Niña

🚢 The Pinta

🚢 The Santa Maria

★ ★ ★

D

If you got this wrong, you are dumber than

77%

of America!

FUN FACTS

For Columbus's first voyage to the New World, he had three ships staffed by 90 sailors. Returning for his second voyage, he sailed with 17 ships loaded with more than 1,200 people. Among the voyagers was Juan Ponce de León, who would later become the first European to run his boat into Florida.

Qestion

20

"The Star-Spangled Banner"
is our national anthem.
Let's sing it:

O say, can you see,
by the dawn's early light,
What so proudly we
hailed at the twilight's
last gleaming...

What line comes next?

A:

Whose broad stripes & bright stars, through the perilous fight

★ ★ ★

And if you want to keep singing:

O'er the ramparts we watched, were so gallantly streaming?

And the rockets' red glare, the bombs bursting in air,

Gave proof through the night that our flag was still there.

O say, does that star-spangled banner yet wave

O'er the land of the free, and the home of the braaaaaaavvvvvve.

If you got this wrong, you are dumber than

61%

of America!

FUN FACTS

"The Star-Spangled Banner" actually has three more verses, which continue to wax on about the general awesomeness of the flag. But that's nothing. The Greek national anthem has a world record 158 verses. That's roughly 158 more than you will ever want to hear.

21

Can you name the planets in our solar system?

We'll spot you Earth.

A:

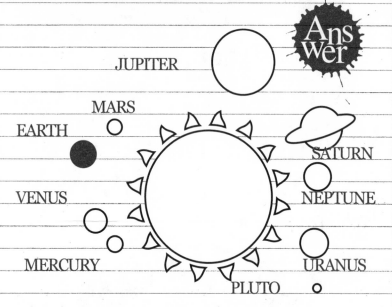

JUPITER

Ans wer

MARS

EARTH

SATURN

VENUS

NEPTUNE

MERCURY

URANUS

PLUTO

Technically, Pluto isn't considered a planet anymore, but it was in your second-grade textbooks, so we're expecting you to remember it. ★ ★ ★

If you got this wrong, you are dumber than

73%

of America!

FUN FACTS

In 2006, astronomers officially defined what qualified as a "planet"—something they'd shockingly never done before. That's when Pluto got the boot. If the astronomers hadn't adopted tight rules, three other newly-discovered floating rocks would have also made the cut, leaving us with a ridiculous 12-planet solar system.

22

Stock market news is almost always accompanied by a report on the change in the

Dow Jones Industrial Average.

Any idea what the Dow actually is?

A:

Ans wer

Let's start with what it's not: It is not a measure of the price of all the stocks on the market. Instead, it's an index that tracks only 30 of the largest public companies in the United States.

★ ★ ★

If you got this wrong, you are dumber than

%

of America!

FUN FACTS

The Dow was created by journalist Charles Dow in 1896 and originally consisted of a mere 12 companies. Of those 12, only General Electric has managed to stay on the list. The power to decide which companies get booted off is held by Charles Dow's other lasting creation—a little paper called *The Wall Street Journal*.

Question

23

Let's revisit
The Civil War.
What was the
first state to >> secede
from the
Union?

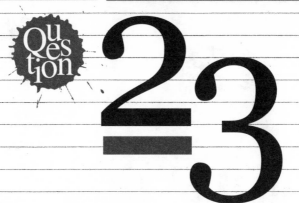

A:

South

Carolina

* * *

If you got this wrong, you are dumber than

%

of America!

FUN FACTS

At the Civil War's first battle, Rebel soldiers pumped 4,000 rounds into the Union-occupied Fort Sumter in South Carolina. There were no casualties, but the North surrendered. As they lowered the U.S. flag, Union troops fired a 100-gun salute—and accidentally killed one of their own soldiers. It was the only death of the battle and the first casualty of the Civil War.

Question

24

This is the outline of a prominent European country.

What country is it?

A:

★ ★ ★

France

If you got this wrong, you are dumber than

35%

of America!

FUN FACTS

During the French Revolution, the government officially ditched the traditional calendar and created a new one in which the months were named after attributes of the seasons. So there were months with names like "Windy," "Snowy" and "Flower." The revolutionaries should have stuck with chopping off heads.

Question 25

The Periodic Table.

You spent an entire year of your life dealing with it in chemistry class. What do the little numbers at the top of every box indicate?

82

LEAD

Pb

207.2

A:

That's the
Atomic Number

It tells you how many protons an element has in its nucleus.

★ ★ ★

If you got this wrong, you are dumber than

61%

of America!

FUN FACTS

The periodic table was developed by Russian chemist Dmitri Ivanovich Mendeleyev. Mendeleyev fell one vote short of winning the 1906 Nobel Prize for his discovery, so, to make up for that slight, chemists dubbed element 101, "Mendelevium." Nice. Any smart schmuck can win a Nobel, but how many people get a metallic, radioactive, transuranic element named after them?

26

On July 4, we wave flags and set off fireworks. But there's a reason the

Fourth

of July

is on the fourth of July. What historic event are we actually celebrating?

A:

The Continental Congress's passage of the
Declaration of Independence

Ans
wer

on July 4, 1776. That's why the holiday is called Independence Day.

★ ★ ★

If you got this wrong, you are dumber than

0.3%

of America!

FUN FACTS

Although the Declaration was officially adopted on July 4, only the Continental Congress's president John Hancock and its secretary signed on that date. Most representatives scribbled their names on August 2, and a few signatures came even later. The final one didn't get added until 1781, a full five years after that first John Hancock.

27

Mt. Everest

straddles two countries.
Name just one.

A:

Nepal & Tibet

Ans wer

(or if you side with the commies,

Nepal & China)

If you got this wrong, you are dumber than

6.3%

of America!

FUN FACTS

The Sherpas who help many climbers summit Mt. Everest frequently have Sherpa as their last name. That's because many of them come from a local tribe of people known as—yup—Sherpas. That tribe even has their own language called—you guessed it—Sherpa.

Question

28

You have to tip
your waitress:
What's 15%
of a $50
check? A:

Ans wer

$7.50

(Although these days it's really kinder to leave 20%, you cheap ass.)

★ ★ ★

If you got this wrong, you are dumber than

 %

of America!

FUN FACTS

The Brits also have trouble calculating funds. All the way up until 1786, the English Royal Treasury tracked its accounts by making notches on sticks. In 1834, they finally got around to burning all the old sticks. Unfortunately, the fire got out of control and burned down the entire Parliament building.

Question

29

Sacagawea
was important enough to our country's history to make her way onto the dollar coin.
What was it she did again?

A:

She served as a translator and
guide to Lewis and Clark as
they crossed America.
Oh, and she did it all
with a baby on her back!

★ ★ ★

If you got this
wrong, you are
dumber than

78%

of America!

FUN FACTS

Don't worry if you're used to
spelling Sacagawea's name as
Sacajawea or even Sakakawea—no
one knows for sure what's correct.
Not even Lewis and Clark. Check
their journals from the trip and
you'll find her name spelled 14
different ways.

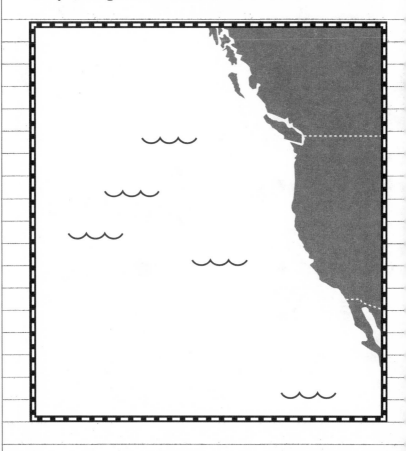

QuEstion 30

Here's the left side of our
continent. Generally speaking...

Where the hell's Hawaii?

Put your finger about where it should be.

Ans wer

Hawaii

We'll give you credit for putting

your finger anywhere in this circle.

★ ★ ★

If you got this wrong, you are dumber than

36%

of America!

FUN FACTS

Captain James Cook was the first European to stumble across the Hawaiian islands. At the time, he named them the Sandwich Islands, after his benefactor John Montague, the fourth Earl of Sandwich. Awesomely, this is the same Earl of Sandwich who once slapped some meat between two slices of bread, thus inventing the sandwich.

Question 31

The Impressionist painters are among history's most popular:

- **Monet**
- **Renoir**
- **Cézanne**
- **Degas**

You know you've heard of them, but can you give a first name for even one of them?

A:

Claude Monet
Pierre-Auguste Renoir
Paul Cézanne
Edgar Degas

> (Actually, Degas's full first name was
> Hilaire-Germain-Edgar, but not even his
> mom bothered with that whole mouthful.)

★ ★ ★

**If you got this
wrong, you are
dumber than**

%

of America!

FUN FACTS

Cézanne—whose work formed a
bridge between Impressionism and
Cubism—won wide acclaim during
his lifetime. But his biggest fan was
probably his pet. He taught his
parrot to squawk, "Cézanne is a
great painter!" which the bird did
with regularity.

32

When

Jackie Robinson

made his Major League Baseball debut in 1947, it shattered a massive racial barrier and changed American culture.

Any idea what team he played for?

A:

The Dodgers

back when they were
in Brooklyn

★ ★ ★

**If you got this
wrong, you are
dumber than**

%

of America!

FUN FACTS

Robinson played his entire career
for the Dodgers. In fact, the day
he received a call telling him he'd
been traded to the Giants was
the same day he signed a secret
agreement to leave baseball for a
corporate job. His bizarre choice
of new employer? The coffee
company Chock Full o'Nuts.

Question

33

Plants are pretty important because they do a little something called photosynthesis.

What is photosynthesis?

A:

It's a chemical process that uses the energy from light to turn water and carbon dioxide into oxygen and sugar. Basically:

Sunlight becomes food

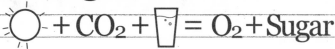

$$\text{(sun)} + CO_2 + \text{(water)} = O_2 + \text{Sugar}$$

>

* * *

If you got this wrong, you are dumber than

%

of America!

FUN FACTS

Due to photosynthesis, a single tree produces almost 260 pounds of oxygen per year. Plant an acre of trees, and they'll remove 2.6 tons of carbon dioxide from the atmosphere per year. Meanwhile, there is absolutely nothing you do that is even remotely as productive.

Question

34

Just like the U.S., **Mexico** is divided up into states. There are 31 of them!

Can you name even one?

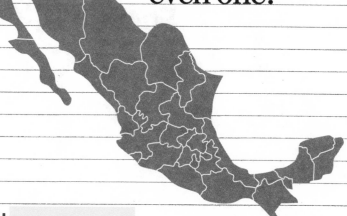

A:

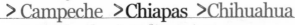

> Aguascalientes
  > Baja California
    >Baja California Sur
> Campeche >Chiapas >Chihuahua
    >Coahuila >Colima >Durango
> Guanajuato >Guerrero >Hidalgo >Jalisco
    >Mexico >Michoacán >Morelos >Nayarit
>Nuevo León >Oaxaca >Puebla >Querétaro
>Quintana Roo >San Luis Potosí >Sinaloa
 >Sonora >Tabasco >Tamaulipas
   >Tlaxcala >Veracruz >Yucatán
                >Zacatecas

★ ★ ★

If you got this
wrong, you are
dumber than

 %

of America!

FUN FACTS

Yes, one of the states is named
Chihuahua. And yes, that's where
the runty dogs were discovered
and got their name. So yes, it was
completely factually accurate when
the Taco Bell Chihuahua spoke
Spanish and went crazy
for chalupas.

Question

35

Impeachment

is the act of bringing a president to trial in front of Congress—not actually booting him out of office.

Only two presidents in the history of the U.S. have been impeached. One was Bill Clinton.

Who was the other?

A:

Andrew Johnson

(Richard Nixon resigned before he could be impeached.)

If you got this wrong, you are dumber than

28%

of America!

FUN FACTS

In an extremely politically motivated move, Johnson was impeached for trying to fire his secretary of war. The Senate fell one vote short of drop-kicking Johnson from office, and he didn't run for re-election. Instead he eventually became a senator, making him the only former president to serve in the Senate.

Question

36

What is the current Pope's name?

A:

The current pontiff was born
Joseph Ratzinger

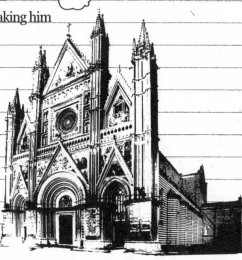

He took Benedict as his
special pope name, making him
Pope Benedict XVI

We'll accept either.

★ ★ ★

If you got this wrong, you are dumber than

74%

of America!

FUN FACTS

In 1378, it was even harder to know the pope's name—because there were two of them. After electing Pope Urban VI, the cardinals changed their mind and picked Pope Clement VII. Both men claimed to be the real pope, both excommunicated the other and neither backed down. So for 40 years, the world had rival popes.

Question

37

Do you have any concept of pre-historic times? Roughly how long ago did

dinosaurs

walk the planet?

 a) 1 million years ago

 b) 10 million years ago

 c) 100 million years ago

 d) 1 billion years ago

A:

> C)

100 million years ago

The first dinosaurs appeared about 230 million years ago and then they all bit the dust about 65 million years ago.

★ ★ ★

If you got this wrong, you are dumber than

%

of America!

FUN FACTS

Extinction is a pretty hard thing to avoid. Scientists estimate that some 30 billion different species of organisms have existed during Earth's 4.5 billion-year lifespan. Of those species, 99.99% have become extinct. So go ahead and spew out those greenhouse gases. Our chances aren't looking too good, anyway.

Question 38

Who was the U.S. president during World War I?

A:

Woodrow Wilson

If you got this wrong, you are dumber than

33%

of America!

FUN FACTS

When WWI broke out in 1914, Wilson followed the will of U.S. citizens and actually refused to join the battle. In fact, he ran for re-election in 1916 with the campaign slogan, "He Kept Us Out of War." But like all effective campaign promises, that one was soon broken.

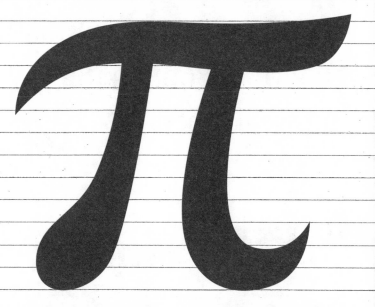

Hey look, here's pi.

What number is that equal to?

A:

3.141592653589793
2384626433832795
0288419716939937510
5820974944592307816406
28620899862803482534...

But we'll accept 3.14

★ ★ ★

If you got this wrong, you are dumber than

82%

of America!

FUN FACTS

German mathematician Ludolph van Ceulen was the first to calculate pi to 53 digits. He was so proud of his accomplishment that when he died in 1610, he actually had the number written on his tombstone. That must have been one very large, very boring tombstone.

Question

40

You know that

Bill of Rights

thing that got tacked on to
the Constitution? It is made
up of 10 amendments.

Name three.

A:

First Amendment: **Freedom of speech. Freedom of the press. Freedom of religion & freedom to peaceable assembly.**
Second Amendment: **The right to bear arms.**
Third Amendment: **Protection from the quartering of troops.**
Fourth Amendment: **Protection from unreasonable search and seizure.**
Fifth Amendment: **Provisions concerning due process of the law, such as the freedom from being forced to testify against oneself and the prohibition against trying an individual twice for the same crime, a.k.a. double jeopardy.**
Sixth Amendment: **Guarantee of a speedy public trial in the district where the crime was committed.**
Seventh Amendment: **Guarantee of trial by jury in civil cases.**
Eighth Amendment: **Prohibition of excessive bail and cruel and unusual punishment.**
Ninth Amendment: **Proclamation that citizens have basic human rights even if they haven't been specifically mentioned in the Constitution.**
Tenth Amendment: **Edict that powers not given to the national government by the Constitution are reserved for the states or people.**

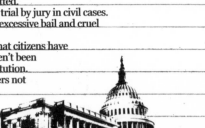

★ ★ ★

If you got this wrong, you are dumber than

%

of America!

FUN FACTS

The Bill of Rights initially contained 12 amendments. The original first amendment dealt with how to allocate seats in Congress, and it was never ratified. The original second amendment dealt with Congressional pay increases, and it did eventually get ratified—but not until 200 years later. It is now the 27th amendment.

Question

41

Albert Einstein famously created the equation:

$$e = mc^2$$

Can you name what those letters stand for?

A:

Answer

energy   mass

↓   ↓

$e=mc^2$

↑

the speed of light

D

If you got this wrong, you are dumber than

51%

of America!

FUN FACTS

Einstein's formula basically says that matter and energy are the same thing. In fact, the body of an average-sized adult contains enough potential energy to explode with the force of 30 hydrogen bombs. We're guessing that explosion would be triggered by eating bean burritos. *Hey-O!*

Question

42

Name one novel written by Ernest Hemingway.

A:

> The Old Man and the Sea
>> The Sun Also Rises
>>> A Farewell to Arms
> For Whom the Bell Tolls > **To Have and Have Not**
>> The Torrents of Spring > Death in the Afternoon
>>> **Green Hills of Africa** > The Garden of Eden
> Across the River and Into the Trees
>> A Moveable Feast
> The Dangerous Summer
> Islands in the Stream

Answer

* * *

If you got this
wrong, you are
dumber than

75%

of America!

FUN FACTS

Hemingway was known for being
aggressively masculine—maybe
because he was overcompensating.
His mother had always wanted
twins, so when Ernie was young,
she would dress him and his sister
in identical skirts and bonnets and
tell strangers the two were twin
girls. Sometimes she'd even call
him "Ernestine."

Question

43

The Statue of Liberty
is one of the most iconic symbols
of our country, but we didn't build
the old broad ourselves.

What country gave her to us?

A:

> France

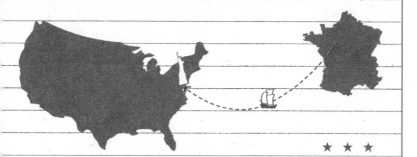

★ ★ ★

If you got this wrong, you are dumber than

96%

of America!

FUN FACTS

The Statue of Liberty's internal skeletal support system was designed by Eiffel Tower creator Gustave Eiffel. The statue was originally intended to act as a lighthouse, but that didn't last. Although the torch keeps the light of freedom alive, it is a touch too dim to keep ships from wrecking on U.S. shores.

Question 44

Islam

has become a key shaper of world events. Do you even know roughly when that religion first began?

A) 200 B.C.

B) 200 A.D.

C) 600 A.D.

D) 1200 A.D.

A:

★ ★ ★

600 A.D.

| 200 B.C. | 200 A.D. | 600 A.D. | 1200 A.D. |

Islam
Begins

If you got this wrong, you are dumber than

%

of America!

FUN FACTS

The vicious sectarian split between the Sunnis and Shiites traces its roots all the way back to arguments over how to choose a new leader after the death of Muhammad in 632 A.D. What's at stake? Muhammad himself is quoted as saying, "My community will break up into 73 [sects], and all of them will be in hellfire except one." Rough.

Question **45**

The conflict in Iraq has dominated news headlines for years.

Iraq has two official languages.

Can you name either

A:

Answer

> # Arabic & Kurdish

★ ★ ★

★

If you got this
wrong, you are
dumber than

60%

of America!

FUN FACTS

Props go to the ancient Iraqis for the creation of writing. More than 5,000 years ago, a civilization known as the Sumerians developed a system that was originally used to track economic transactions. Still, you know it was only a matter of time before some Sumerian wiseass started jotting down dirty jokes.

Do you remember how to multiply fractions?
Solve this simple problem:

$$\frac{1}{6} \times \frac{1}{3} = \boxed{}$$

A)1/2   B)1/9   C)1/18   >

Answer

$$\frac{1}{18}$$ ✓

If you got this wrong, you are dumber than

64%

of America!

FUN FACTS

Our modern day numbers (known as the Hindu-Arabic system) trace their origins as far back as the third century B.C. in India. But it wasn't until the 11th century A.D. that Europeans finally learned the system. Until then they'd used Roman numerals, which scholars now agree are good for little besides numbering Super Bowls.

Question

47

In what month is Martin Luther King Jr. Day?

A:

Ans wer

>>

January

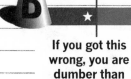

If you got this wrong, you are dumber than

55%

of America!

FUN FACTS

If you missed this question, you are not only dumb—you are also a racist.

Question

48

In WWII, the good guys were called the Allies and the bad guys were called the Axis. In WWI, the good guys were also called the Allies, but the bad guys had a different name.

What were Germany and its partners called in WWI ?

A:

Ans wer

★ ★ ★

The Central Powers

If you got this wrong, you are dumber than

10%

of America!

FUN FACTS

German ruler Kaiser Wilhelm II was related to the royalty of many of the European nations he went to war against—particularly King George V of the U.K. and Tsar Nicholas II of Russia. Those three were close enough that they called each other Willy, Georgie and Nicky.

Question 49

Mexico is directly south of the U.S. There are two countries directly south of Mexico. Can you name either one?

A:

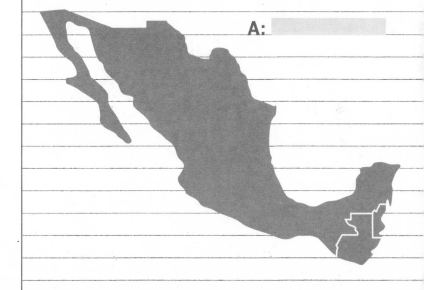

Ans wer

Guatemala and Belize

If you got this wrong, you are dumber than

%

of America!

FUN FACTS

Belize is the only Central American country with English as its official language. Why? Because some of its earliest colonizers were English pirates. How awesome: A nation of pirates! We assume that also means the country's official bird is the parrot, its national flag is a skull and crossbones and its favorite letter of the alphabet is "Arrrrrrr."

Question 50

What religion is the Dalai Lama?

A:

Buddhist
specifically Tibetan Buddhist

★ ★ ★

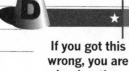

If you got this wrong, you are dumber than

71%

of America!

FUN FACTS

Followers of the current Dalai Lama believe he's the 14th in a line of reincarnations of Chenrezig, the Buddha of compassion. He was discovered at age 3, after he recognized people and things from the life of the 13th Dalai Lama. He even mentioned where Lama 13 kept his dentures. And if that's not proof of divinity, we don't know what is.

51

What started with the words,

"Four score and seven years ago..."

A:

Answer

Abraham Lincoln's speech

"The Gettysburg Address"

★ ★ ★

If you got this wrong, you are dumber than

74%

of America!

FUN FACTS

In addition to giving some pretty decent speeches and winning the freakin' Civil War, Lincoln is also notable for being the only president to ever hold a patent. His invention? A contraption designed to lift riverboats over sandbars. Good thing he stuck with politics.

Question 52

* * *

Charlie Chaplin

is the most
famous
comedic
actor of
all time.
Name just
one of
his films.

A:

>

★ ★ ★

His best known films are:

> **The Kid** > The Circus
> City Lights >**Modern Times**
> **Easy Street** > Limelight
> **The Great Dictator**
> A Woman of Paris
> **The Gold Rush**
> The Tramp

If you listed anything else, you're
probably wrong, but you can double
check yourself at www.imdb.com.

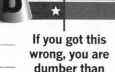

If you got this
wrong, you are
dumber than

%

of America!

FUN FACTS

Chaplin's mustache was a fake,
and he used the exact same one
for 15 years, vowing that if he ever
lost it, he'd never sport lip fuzz on
film again. It's rumored that Adolf
Hitler copied the look because
he thought Chaplin was hilarious.
And if anyone knew comedy, it
was Hitler.

53

We don't expect you to know who's in charge of Canada these days. But do you even know what the guy's title is?

A:

Prime Minister

* * *

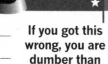

If you got this wrong, you are dumber than

of America!

FUN FACTS

What kind of weighty issues face the prime minister of Canada? Well, Canada's current prime minister, Stephen Harper, has had the courage to tackle the thorny topic of homeless pets. He has devoted part of his Web site to publicizing his cause and even uses his residence as a foster home for kittens.

The most famous line written by

William Shakespeare is:

"To be, or not to be: That is the question."

What character uttered it?

A:

Hamlet

If you got this wrong, you are dumber than 05% of America!

FUN FACTS

The best line that Shakespeare ever penned for something other than a play can be found in his will, where he wrote, "I give unto my wife my second-best bed." It could be that Mrs. Shakespeare got only the second-best bed because, in those days, the best one was reserved for guests. Or it could be that Big Willy knew how to craft an insult even in death.

55

Do you have
any concept of
the metric
system?

Which is longer:
a mile or a
kilometer?

A:

A mile

It takes 1.6 kilometers to make a mile. >>

Point A ———————————————————————————— Point B

★ ★ ★

If you got this wrong, you are dumber than

 %

of America!

FUN FACTS

When created, the meter was originally defined as 1/10,000,000 of the distance between the equator and the North Pole. Now it's officially defined as the distance light travels in a vacuum in 1/299,792,458 of a second. Granted, the size is still the same, but now it seems much more complicated.

56

On what continent can you find the Mojave Desert?

A:

North America

Ans wer

It is better known as the stretch of hotness that includes Death Valley & Las Vegas. ★ ★ ★

If you got this wrong, you are dumber than

52%

of America!

FUN FACTS

The Mojave also holds Joshua Tree National Park, which was where musician Gram Parsons would often go to do drugs. After Parsons ODed in 1973, his friends stole his dead body and smuggled it into the park—where they memorialized him by setting it on fire. A park ranger then stumbled upon the flaming corpse.

57

This is the

Quadratic Formula:

$$x = \frac{-b \pm \sqrt{b^2 - 4ac}}{2a}$$

It was a big deal back when you took algebra. Can you even remember what it was used for?

A:

It was used to solve equations where a variable was raised to the second power. Those equations would have looked like this:

$$ax^2 + bx + c = 0$$

* * *

You could also attempt to solve those equations by factoring or completing the square, but let's be honest: You don't even know what those terms mean anymore.

If you got this wrong, you are dumber than

17%

of America!

FUN FACTS

The equal sign was created by a mathematician living in, of all places, Wales. In 1510, pasty Welshman Robert Recorde busted out the new notation. Previously, math nerds had used two vertical parallel lines to note when two things were equivalent, or they wrote the letters ae. That was short for "aequalis," the Latin word for "equals."

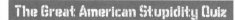

58

The Constitution didn't go into effect until 1788.

Before that, the U.S. operated under the guidelines of a different document. What was that scrap of paper called?

A:

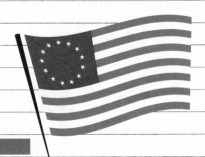

The Articles of Confederation

★ ★ ★

D

If you got this
wrong, you are
dumber than

39%

of America!

FUN FACTS

Written at a time when the new
states were wary of a powerful
central government, the Articles of
Confederation gave very limited powers
to the federal government. For example,
the feds couldn't levy any taxes; they
could merely ask the states for money.
Not surprisingly, not every state always
ponied up. The worst was Georgia,
which never sent a dime.

59

Do you have any concept of
when old people lived?

Who came first:
Plato or Jesus?

A:

Plato

Ans wer

He was born around 427 B.C. That B.C. happens to stand for "Before Christ."

★ ★ ★

If you got this wrong, you are dumber than

%

of America!

FUN FACTS

Plato's real name was Aristocles. "Plato" was a nickname, which roughly translates to "wide shoulders." This could either be a reference to the weight of knowledge Plato bore, or maybe it was just the polite Greek way of saying the dude was fat.

Question 60

Here's a map of Africa.
Label any two countries.
(South Africa doesn't count.)

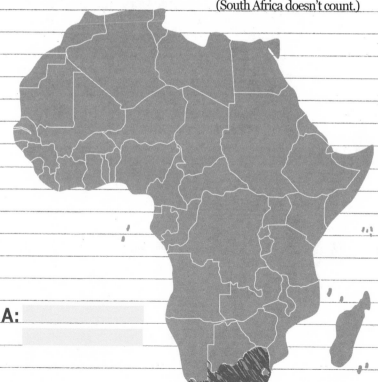

A:

South Africa
(No points. Too easy.)

Tunisia

Morocco

Algeria   Libya   Egypt

Western Sahara

Mauritania

Senegal   Mali   Niger   Chad   Sudan   Eritrea

Gambia

Guinea   Guinea   Burkina   Djibouti

Bissau   Faso   Nigeria   Central   Ethiopia

Sierra Leone   African

Liberia   Benin   Republic   Somalia

Ivory Coast   Ghana   Togo   Uganda   Kenya   Rwanda

Cameroon   Democratic   Burundi   Seychelles

Sao Tome   Republic of   Tanzania

& Principe   the Congo   Malawi

Equatorial   Comoros

Guinea   Angola   Zambia   Mayotte

Zimbabwe   Madagascar

Gabon   Namibia

Republic of   Botswana   Mozambique   Mauritius

the Congo   Swaziland   Reunion

Lesotho

Ans wer

If you got this
wrong, you are
dumber than

57%

of America!

FUN FACTS

In the late 19th century, Europe
conquered much of Africa. The Africans
were armed with muskets, which fired
one round per minute. Meanwhile, the
Europeans had machine guns, which
fired 11 rounds per *second*. At one
1898 battle, British forces mowed down
10,800 Sudanese with the gun. Number
of British dead: 49.

Qestion

61 Obviously, John F. Kennedy & Abraham Lincoln were assassinated while in office, but so were two other U.S. presidents. Can you name either one of them?

Lincoln

Kennedy

A:

Garfield

★ ★ ★

McKinley

★ ★ ★

If you got this
wrong, you are
dumber than

%

of America!

FUN FACTS

Garfield lay dying for 80 days,
during which time 16 doctors tried
unsuccessfully to find and remove
the assassin's bullet. Even telephone
inventor Alexander Graham Bell gave
it a go with an early metal detector, but
the thing kept malfunctioning. That's
probably because the president was
lying on a metal bed—and no one
thought to mention that fact to Bell.

Question

62

How many degrees are in a triangle?

A) **90°**

B) **180°**

C) **270°**

D) **360°**

A:

How Dumb Are You?

Answer

A) ~~90°~~

B) **180°** ✓

C) ~~270°~~

D) ~~360°~~

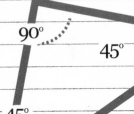

90°
45°
45°

If you got this wrong, you are dumber than **73%** of America!

FUN FACTS

The Pythagorean Theorem, which calculates the leg sizes of right triangles, was created by Greek mathematician Pythagoras. Pythagoras is also credited with coining the word "mathematics." Impressive, but he also swore that his father was the sun god Apollo. His math was a bit off on that one.

The Wright brothers had the first manned, mechanical flying machine. They also had first names. Cough 'em up.

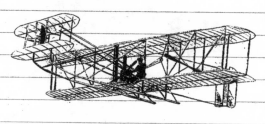

A:

Ans
wer

Orville & Wilbur Wright

★ ★ ★

D

★

If you got this
wrong, you are
dumber than

%

of America!

FUN FACTS

After their historic flight, the Wright
brothers went on to set another
milestone, becoming the first to fly
with passengers. And one of those
passengers, a gentleman by the
name of Thomas Selfridge, set a
record of his own. He became the
first man to ever die from injuries
suffered in a plane crash. Way to go,
Wright brothers!

Question

64

We all know 32 degrees Fahrenheit is the temperature at which water freezes, but at what temperature does it boil?

(Note: Answering in Celsius is considered both cheating & lame.)

O

A:

Answer

212°

★ ★ ★

If you got this wrong, you are dumber than

29%

of America!

FUN FACTS

Thermometer lover Daniel Fahrenheit actually intended for the freezing temperature of water to sit at 30 degrees on his scale. Except he measured wrong. He also thought that the human body temperature would come in at 90—not 98.6—degrees. For a guy who created a measuring system, he wasn't very good at using a measuring system.

Question 65

Only two cities in the world have ever had an atomic bomb dropped on them. The first was Hiroshima.

What was the other?

A:

Nagasaki

If you got this wrong, you are dumber than

74%

of America!

In 1951, the Atomic Energy Commission began testing atomic devices in the Nevada desert, a mere 65 miles from Las Vegas. Vegas, being Vegas, made the most of it by holding bomb viewing parties, where tourists could get sauced while waiting for a nuclear flash. Soon, mushroom clouds had been added to casino advertisements and even the county's official seal.

So... How Dumb Are You?

It's the moment of truth. For an overarching view of the true breadth and depth of your ignorance, count the total number of questions you missed; then consult the following scale of shame:

Subhuman

More than 45 wrong

Let's start with the good news: You are smarter than all inanimate objects and the vast majority of plant life. The bad news: If you were ever a contestant on *Jeopardy!*, you would be beaten by a trained seal. Some other thoughts: We're guessing you had this quiz read to you, because with a score this low you are likely either illiterate or in a coma. So you obviously have friends willing to interact with you. Which is sweet. Nonetheless, your score indicates a level of intelligence so minuscule that we advise you to refrain from some normal human tasks, such as operating any machine that requires electricity. And attempting to pronounce words with multiple syllables. And breeding. This critique of your intelligence may come across as harsh, but please don't take the comments personally. It's not your fault that your mother drank when she was pregnant.

Challenged

From 30-44 wrong

They say those who don't know history are doomed to repeat it. In your case, you're so ignorant of history that you'll never even realize what you're repeating. So here's hoping ignorance is bliss. That being said, you should probably never be allowed to vote. Or speak in public. Given your level of learning, you'll find yourself most comfortable when having conversations with children 10 and younger. But try to avoid that: talking to you will actually make the children stupider. And it's not your job to impede the intellectual development of our youth. That's what public schools are for. You should be utterly ashamed of your performance on this test, unless, of course, you were taking it while suffering from a handicap. This is a very respectable score if you have Alzheimer's.

Ignorant

From 15-29 wrong

You are a living, breathing example of why our country is lagging behind other industrialized nations. While you probably attended at least elementary school, we're guessing you were either asleep and/or drunk for most of the experience. Still, when it comes to employment, you are amply qualified for any job that requires heavy lifting, repetitive movements or making change for bills smaller than $20. You may also want to consider the lucrative field of migrant labor. When it comes to your personal life, it is theoretically possible that you may someday find an equally unintelligent person to marry. Good luck with that. Just be careful about having children. If those youngsters ever make it to high school, they will officially be smarter than you.

Uninformed

From 1-14 wrong

You have clearly completed some form of schooling. Unfortunately, every year since your graduation you have actually grown dumber. Hopefully, the book learning that is no longer in your skull has been replaced with knowledge that's more relevant to your daily life: for example, how to change the oil in your car or manage your 401(k). What's that? You don't know how to do those things either? You're a cretin. Still, this is America, and we can pay other people (often born in foreign countries) to do most of our work for us. So you'll most likely lead a happy life and find someone tolerable to settle down with. Intelligence isn't everything. We're sure you have a wonderful personality.

Average

0 wrong

Bravo, you have managed to retain the base level of knowledge expected of any mature adult in modern society. You are intellectually adequate. You are demonstrably *non*-retarded. You are not (yet) an embarrassment to your parents. Obviously, we can't assert that you are actually intelligent. Such judgments are beyond the scope of this quiz, which was designed solely to identify and brand the truly stupid. There are no winners here, only non-losers. And at least, in this one small time and place, you are a non-loser. Lukewarm congratulations!